Date Due

JAN - 5 1979		MAR 2 3 1992	
JAN 29 1979			
MAY 1 - 1979			
MAY 5 1979		NOV 2 0 1993	
AUG 3 1 1979		NOV 1 7 '98	
OCT 18 1979		JUL 2 3 1999	
MAR 13 1981		APR 0 6 2004	
JUN 2 1 1982			
MAR 1 7 1983			
MAR 2 9 1983			
OCT - 9 1984			
JAN 0 3 1987			
FEB 12 1988			
FEB 2 6 1988			
JAN 1 6 1989			

658   Priamo, Carol, 1947-
.874   The general store.   Toronto, McGraw-
09713   Hill Ryerson, 1978.
Pri   104 p.   illus.

1. General stores - Ontario.
I. Title.
007082780X   0633844

6/EX/CN

THE GENERAL STORE

THE GENERAL STORE

Text and photographs
by Carol Priamo

McGraw-Hill Ryerson Limited

**Toronto   Montreal   New York   St. Louis   San Francisco
Auckland   Beirut   Bogotá   Düsseldorf   Johannesburg
Lisbon   London   Lucerne   Madrid   Mexico   New Delhi
Panama   Paris   San Juan   São Paulo   Singapore   Sydney   Tokyo**

ISBN 0-07-082780-X

Design: Carol Priamo

1 2 3 4 5 6 7 8 9 10 BP 7 6 5 4 3 2 1 0 9 8

Printed and bound in Canada

To Hope and Shelagh

Crosby's Store, Uxbridge, in the late 1890s.
(Ontario Archives, S 15405.)

Contents

Preface

As a child in Guelph, one of my favourite things to do was to visit Rex Bartlett's corner store. Bartlett's wasn't a real "general store", but it had enough variety to capture my curiosity and amuse me even before I was big enough to see over the candy counter. In those days the walk of a few blocks seemed quite a journey, but it was worth it to be able to "hang around" with my brother at the soda fountain, or to rummage through piles of comic books—while the other regulars sat around drinking coffee and chatting with Rex.

Years later while travelling the back roads of rural Ontario researching another book, I rediscovered the joys of the general store—some glorified corner stores like Bartlett's and some general stores in the true sense. To enter one meant finding a temporary refuge from the solitary and tiring road, for here, comfortable and unrushed, I could browse among shelves of things I hadn't seen since Grandmother's house. And I could buy apples and nuts right from the barrel.

The bell on the door rang customers in and out, and presiding over this storehouse of memories was the shopkeeper, a perfect stranger, yet someone I felt I had known all my life.

Times are hard for the rural merchant, and sometimes it is a struggle to hang on to this small empire of commodities which has been his life and possibly his father's before him. But the appeal remains. The general store is a place to explore and discover—like searching for treasure in an old attic. Always different, always familiar, it is a fun place that appeals to the kid in us as though we were still eye-level with the candy jars.

For the past two years, I have concentrated on visiting general stores in Ontario in order to capture in words and pictures the many endearing qualities of the shops and their keepers. This book is for those who remember with fondness the general store they knew and for those storekeepers who keep that memory alive in the general stores they won't give up.

The General Store Then And Now

The General Store In The Past

From the beginning of settlement in Ontario in the late eighteenth century, the general store has played a vital role in providing its community with the material goods necessary for comfort and survival. The general store was often one of the first structures to appear, and in many areas continued to be the only sign of mercantile activity. The development of such stores in the province cannot be described in a purely chronological manner, but the essential point is that while some stores remained virtually unchanged in their appearance, type of goods stocked, and services provided, other modest establishments underwent great change. Their decline or success, of course, depended on a number of factors.

Before 1820 in those counties not accessible to trade on Lake Ontario, of the few stores that were built, many survived only a short time. Imported goods were scarce. Abhorrent road conditions inhibited the transport of available goods and limited the mobility of the small number of potential customers. It was difficult to build a business when local produce was not yet available in sufficient quantity from recently settled farmers. Several years of cultivation would be necessary before the land yielded crops and supported livestock for trade at the general store.

The period between 1820 and 1840 saw a transition from rudimentary settlement to the emergence of a feasible mercantile situation. Young men with enterprising spirit had the foresight to understand the financial implications of a growing population, increased availability of goods from local farmers and small

Porch, Rosser General Store, Denfield.

manufacturers, and improved transportation. They also had the initiative and ambition to use the situation to advantage.

An item in the *Colonial Advocate* of March 8, 1827, illustrates this point:

"Young men often begin business here without any capital at all; they find security or are known in Montreal [the importing centre of the country], consequently obtain credit. . . . These young men then establish themselves either in villages or in places where they have the fewest competitors or capital; and they sell their stock to the country farmer for . . . articles of produce, or on credit, for a promise of payment in produce the following winter. . . . They [the merchants] built grist and saw mills, distilleries and potash works, and pay the workmen chiefly in trade, that is, in goods."

After 1850, stores became more numerous and better stocked with the increase in locally manufactured goods. The continuing improvement of roads, the introduction of the railway system, and the increase of a cash flow also contributed to the success of the general store.

In his book *The Store that Timothy Built*, William Stephenson writes that in the 1860s:

"There were more than 2,000 general stores in Ontario alone as many as in all the rest of Canada combined. Each one usually shared village space with a water-powered grist (flour) mill, a blacksmith's shop, a few houses, a church, a school and an inn or tavern. The character of the proprietor decided whether the centre of social life was to be the inn or the store."

In large towns there were often a dozen stores as well as several general stores: drugstores, bookstores, hardware stores, bakeries and jewellery shops. Often a prosperous general merchant might abandon his small establishment and move his business into a newly constructed large building which he would divide into two shops such as a grocery store and hardware store. He would own the stores but hire others to manage them giving him free time for other ventures.

This proliferation had the effect of affording the customer a greater choice of goods, but it forced the merchant into a highly competitive position. Merchants vied bitterly for potentially

(Opposite)
Store of George Duncan, Drummondville, Ontario (1876). This simple example is representative of the modest general store which, despite the existence of bigger stores, was still a common feature late in the century. This type is still seen on the backroads of the province.
(From Historical Atlas of the Counties of Lincoln and Welland, *Toronto, 1876.)*

J. Kidd & Sons Importers & General Dealers, Dublin, Ontario (1879). With the growing prosperity of some general merchants, the modest general store could become more elaborate, such as this example of J. Kidd & Sons Importers & General Dealers in Dublin. This shop displays a more grand external appearance as well as a spacious and well-stocked interior. Unlike the simple general store, it has a lower floor for boots, shoes, and crockery. This store obviously reflects the success of an enterprising family.
(From Illustrated Historical Atlas of Perth County, *Toronto, 1879.)*

prosperous sites in newly planned towns.

Some general merchants flourished under these conditions of vigorous activity, even managing to specialize or to expand. Others, however, were pushed out of the market. Rural stores fared better than those on the outskirts of town which lost their trade to the larger centre.

The introduction of the railway, which was instrumental in bolstering many businesses, had an opposite effect on the business of stores in towns that it bypassed. The same was true of improved roads which tended to link only those centres that had already attained a degree of prosperity. With the railway enabling products from large urban manufacturers to reach out-lying districts, local manufacturers who could no longer compete began to dwindle. The general merchant decreased his direct trade with local manufacturers and took on an increased function as part of the distribution system. Thus his role became more specialized. Competition became more fierce; for example, a great blow to the general store was the introduction of the mail-order business with the issue of Eaton's first catalogue in 1884 followed by other catalogues, such as Simpsons'. Goods of any description could be obtained more efficiently; variety was greater; and quality was assured.

Increased urbanization, centralized manufacturing, improved distribution, and other factors changed the need for the general store and altered the type of goods it could successfully handle. Services previously offered were sometimes replaced by specialized industries and establishments such as banks and the post office. Though these conditions did not adversely affect all stores, some found themselves in a very precarious position, and many were relegated to simple grocery stores or went out of business entirely.

Barclay's Block, Georgetown.
This "general store" is the nineteenth-century equivalent of the modern-day shopping plaza. It is the general store converted into specialized shops creating a commercial block. A very prosperous storeowner often seized the opportunity of an advantageous location and a growing population and bought a large building which he then divided into shops; each shop stocked only one type of article.
(From Illustrated Historical Atlas of Halton County, *Toronto, 1877.)*

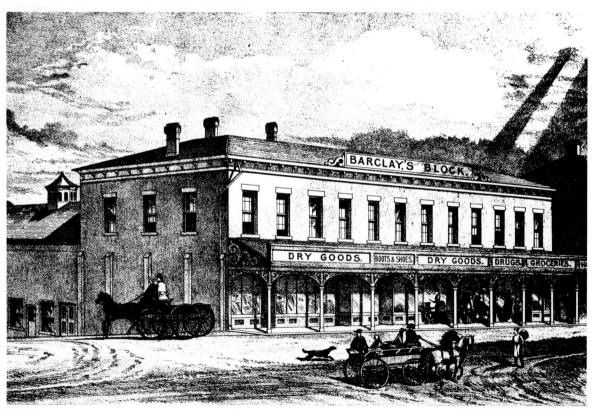

HOW IT LOOKED

General stores in the first half of the nineteenth century were fairly uniform in design and had several common features. The size of the building and the amount of decorative detail varied. Most were simple houses, one and a half storeys high with a pitched roof. But unlike the domestic edifice, the store in most cases was turned so that the short wall or gable end faced the street. The lower shop windows were large in order to light the deep narrow interior and to allow passersby to peek in. The upper windows (usually two) were smaller and placed directly and symmetrically over the lower windows. There was a central doorway to the store which was accessible by wooden steps and porch. The porch was usually raised a good distance above ground level not only to elevate the entrance of the store above the muddy or dusty roads, but to provide a platform for the loading and unloading of goods from buckboards and wagons. The

An early photograph of the T.A. Austin & Co. general store and post office at Chapleau, shows the owners with their goods displayed on the porch. This building also housed a barber shop (right).
(Ontario Archives, S 15715.)

(Overleaf)
This general store, photographed in the early twentieth century, exhibits a most interesting facade with its unusually-shaped false front, its comparatively long entrance stairs and the stocky pillars supporting the overhang. In this store, the post office and shop are separate. It was located in Lambton Mills.
(Ontario Archives, S 16100.)

15

lower facade was often adorned with a perma-
nent awning supported by simple or elaborately
turned posts. The awnings protected the storekeeper's goods from fading in bright sun, and
also served as a canopy for sheltering chatting
customers in inclement weather. Goods unload-
ed onto the porch would also need protection
until they could be brought into the store. The
upper storey might sport a balcony, either a
partial one or one stretching across the entire
facade. If there was an upper balcony, there was
inevitably an upper central door.

The unadorned store gave an impression of
austerity. But this was lessened in those designs
which added a verandah or balcony or both,
decorative woodwork and brickwork, and, of
course, the familiar store signs.

Not all general stores looked like a house
turned sideways. Many resembled boxes of
various shapes and heights. This was mainly due
to the use of the square false front rising above
and hiding the front gable. This addition to the
traditional design gave the tiny store apparent
height and enhanced its prominence in the
streetscape. This method of making a one or
one-and-one-half storey building look like a
two-storey structure was a common feature on
many early buildings throughout the country
and was not limited to shop architecture. It was
particularly prevalent in the boomtowns of
frontier America and is sometimes referred to as
a boomtown front.

Later, stores became larger to accommodate
the demands of the growing clientele. Although
the general store building followed the architec-
tural trends of the day, that style was always
modified and simplified because the appearance
of the store was secondary to its function. The
interior structure of the shop was equally
simple. It was primarily a wide-open, usually
deep space with the merchant's office in a corner
or at the rear, either open or private. Besides the
stock which cluttered this space, one could find
several crude stools or chairs for relaxing
customers, a fireplace or stove for warmth, and
in the case of larger interiors, two or three
simple columns for support.

The upper storey was used most commonly as
living quarters for the merchant and his family,
but could also be used for storage or some other
function, such as a meeting hall, if the merchant
had his residence elsewhere.

THE GOODS IT STOCKED

Depending on the size of the business and the availability of goods, the stock in early general stores varied in quantity and choice. But for the growing community the general store was the only outlet for material needs, and it catered to these needs as best as possible.

The merchandise carried by the general store was either local produce (mainly grains, potash, dairy products, pork, lumber, and furs) or goods imported from Britain and the United States. In the case of local producers, the storekeeper would trade his imported goods for those brought in from the farmers. In the first half of the nineteenth century money was scarce and this barter system was a convenient and logical way of doing business. Credit was easily established, since trust was essential. The customer had an immediate need for household staples, and the country merchant expected to wait until harvest for payment.

William Brock's General Store in Port Perry, shown here at the turn of the century, demonstrates the variety and quantity of goods available at the general store at this time—everything from fur coats to scrub-brushes. In many stores customers were provided with stools or chairs to relax on while examining the merchandise selected by the clerks from the appropriate shelf.
(Ontario Archives, S 12990.)

(Opposite) Sunday afternoon at the Bethany general store—a modern-day contrast.

In order to obtain the imported goods, the merchant at first travelled to his importers in the province. This merchandise had arrived in barrels, kegs and crates from overseas via Montreal or from New York to ports on Lake Ontario, mainly Toronto and Niagara. When roads improved, salesmen from developing urban centres brought foreign and domestic items to the rural merchant encouraging him to examine and order goods. Later the railway made this network of distribution more complex and more effective. Goods shipped from a distance were, of course, more expensive by the time they reached their destination. And especially in the first half of the nineteenth century there was little choice as to taste or fashion outside of Toronto. One could not be too choosy about the style of one's shoes when purchasing them along with sugar and salt pork in the same store.

Although quantity and variety was often limited, the store was always well stocked with a conglomeration of local produce and import items. Merchandise in a store of the early nineteenth century might include textiles, notions, utensils (made in Quebec forges), tea kettles, hatforms, teas, and dyes. To please the merchants' customers, additional luxury items when available would be included, such as tobacco, pipes, leather goods, exotic cloths, writing materials, spices, coffee, ostrich feathers, ribbons, lace and silk stockings. When local manufacturers became established in the province, the choice and quantity of goods not only became greater but both necessity and luxury items became cheaper.

Most merchandise, whether locally produced or imported, was displayed with little or no packaging on rows of shelves, behind a sizeable counter. If a customer was interested in examining an item he was assisted by the shopkeeper who would retrieve it from the shelves and place it on the counter. In the case of a fussy shopper, the counter would soon become completely littered with a variety of goods before he would make up his mind.

Barrels, kegs and crates, containing produce and other bulk items, were arranged on the floor and customers brought their own baskets and other containers to carry away their purchases. Generally, sugar, flour, salt pork and other household staples were bought in bulk. In one day of shopping, a family might cart home

several barrels and crates of goods which they would keep in their oversized kitchens.

Items extracted from invoices (1800-1812) for goods shipped from Montreal through Kingston to the general store of Thomas Cummings of Chippawa in the Niagara area.

1 piece callico No. 1, 28 yds.	400 quills
2 pieces Irish linen No. 1, 52 yds.	½ doz. slates
	100 slate pencils
2 pieces common white flannel	4 Bibles
	1 Tom Jones 4 vols.
8 lbs. all colored thread No. 10	4 Entick's Dictionary
	2 rugs
½ gross brass thimbles	4 pr. of 3 point blankets
1 doz. women's cotton stockings No. 3	1 doz. rat traps
	6 iron tea kettles
	8 nutmeg graters
9 purple chintz shawls	3 doz. pewter teaspoons
6 pair plated martingale hooks	1 crate crockery
	9 barrels 142 lb. loaf sugar
1 doz. men's tanned gloves	60 lbs. black pepper
2 doz. shirt wires	20 lb. roll brimstone
1 doz. shaving boxes	75 gals. port wine
2 doz. ivory combs	½ doz. shovels
1 doz. paper snuff boxes	3 hand saws
	500 gun flints
6 lbs. red chalk	2 doz. scalping knives
14 Dillworth's spelling books	½ lb. box camphor

By the very nature of settlement early in Canadian history, each community had to be a self-contained little unit. The three most essential people to the self-sufficiency of the community were the farmer, the miller and the storekeeper since they represented the production, processing and distribution of food. But food and other goods were only part of the store's business—essential services were also vital and unobtainable elsewhere.

In a society where money was less important than the exchange of necessary services, a central meeting place where information on supply and demand could be exchanged was critically important. At the general store, partners in various business transactions could meet to discuss dealings of mutual interest. The storekeeper was usually instrumental in the arrangements. For example, a farmer bringing a large amount of produce to the store could build up a sizeable credit balance. If the farmer was in need of a team for plowing, he might be introduced by the merchant to a man who could supply such a team and who would accept as payment the right to draw against the farmer's credit at the store. In this case the merchant was not only acting as a middleman, but was in effect the village banker exercising sole control over the dispensing of credit in the community. When cash became the prevalent medium of exchange, customers could borrow money at the store, and repay with interest, a service banks would offer when they became established later in the century.

General stores contained the local post office since there were no separate post offices before 1850. Mail was brought by stage coach regularly and recipients were charged for the delivery when they picked up their correspondence. So the merchant distributed mail and collected this fee. General stores have through the years continued to offer this service, and today many surviving stores are still the only post office in the vicinity.

Stores before 1850 were often, in effect, a combination store and tavern. Anna Jameson, a British immigrant, in her description of London, Ontario, in 1837 noted:

"Besides the seven taverns there is a number of little grocery stores which are, in fact, drinking houses. And though a law exists,

General stores often provided communication services. After 1880, when the telephone began to appear in communities across Canada, the only accessible telephone was usually located in the general store. This original phone, found today in the Rosser General Store in Denfield, dates from the turn of the century. A litter of yellowed paper remains in the post office of this store. (Overleaf)

which forbids the sale of spiritous liquors in small quantities by any but licensed publicans, they easily contrive to elude the law; as thus: - a customer enters the shop, and asks for two or three penny-worth of nuts, or cakes, and he receives a few nuts, and a large glass of whiskey. The whiskey, you observe, is given, not sold, and no one can swear to the contrary."

This particular ploy and others to the same effect enabled the merchant to run a drinking establishment on his own premises, and he may have received alcohol from the local tavernkeeper in return for goods from his stock. A typical entry in the storekeeper's account book might be the succinct but suggestive note: "Received from Joe Smith, 3 quarts of rye." At any rate, the tavernkeeper did not mind the competition since there seemed to be an inexhaustible demand for liquor, customers at the store often preferring to tipple while selecting their purchases.

In addition to obtaining almost any type of goods, including spirits, and his mail, the customer often could hire horses or oxen at the store if he needed extra ones, or if he wanted the animals for short term use.

Other tradesmen in the village made use of the merchant's services as a concessionaire.

Those who could not afford a shop of their own worked in the store providing customers with services the merchant could not supply himself: tailoring, bootmaking, millinery, and other specialized trades. These tradesmen were paid, as usual, in goods from the store.

Prospective brides and grooms came to the store for a very specialized service, for often the general store merchant had applied for authorization to issue marriage licences and he was only too happy to assist the willing couple—for a fee of course.

From about 1880, the telephone began to appear in communities across Canada. Much-frequented places of business became a natural choice for the first phones, customers coming into the general store to make or receive calls. By 1890, switchboards were coming into use, and they too were often installed in this central location. The operators, of course, knew everybody's business—technology extending the store's role as a place of information exhange.

Supplying goods, lending "money," providing postal and livery service, serving alcohol, providing custom tailoring, bootmaking, millinery and other services, the general store could certainly become the most popular place in the community.

The storekeeper lived in the store, whether above it, or in the rear portion. Or, if he became more affluent he might build a separate house near to or adjoining the shop. He was never far from his place of business and consequently, his hours were flexible, although long by present-day standards. He usually worked fourteen hours a day, six days a week. And when he was busy with deliveries, his wife or son or brother would take over the running of the store. The general store was often a family venture, and stores were usually passed down through several generations. A young son would have the opportunity of serving a lengthy and thorough apprenticeship, acquainting himself with every aspect of the operation before he reached adulthood.

Storekeepers of the nineteenth century were described as gracious hosts, allowing customers to browse for hours. People might sit and chat for half a day about local news, politics, or the state of the year's crops. The storekeeper might offer them some beverage, and when they were ready to leave, it was his custom to wish them farewell while never neglecting to show them to the door and to open it for their convenience.

The storekeeper who was established knew each of his local customers personally. He was aware of the tastes and preferences of individual people, and could, therefore, offer items that were sure to interest, this being both good for sales, and also conducive to future purchases. He might also advise customers as to the use of the items he carried, or, if presented with a particular problem on the part of the customer, he might be able to find among his multitudinous shelves of goods, just the product that would solve the dilemma.

As well as knowing his own people, the shopkeeper was in an ideal position to greet strangers. Sometimes a weary traveller found he could not secure lodgings. The shopkeeper's home became a temporary inn. Newcomers to a town could make the acquaintance of the shopkeeper before meeting any other neighbours, and those who were passing through would occasionally stop for tobacco or a refreshing drink.

Between these contacts and those he made in the trade, the storekeeper's world was a lively one, but he had to be careful as well. Anna

Jameson thought that the qualities of a good storekeeper were "intelligence, activity, and popular manners." Intelligence certainly, he had to know his markets, his suppliers, and the price his goods and services could best obtain. He also had to battle the competition, such as country pedlars who would bring goods at a savings, and who provided personal shop-at-home service. But the most difficult and complex mental activity the storekeeper engaged in was probably his credit dealings. The merchant was involved to a large extent in "international" trade. In the nineteenth century he sold for export, wheat and lumber which he had acquired from local farmers in exchange for goods. Sometimes the goods had left his store long before the farmer or lumberman delivered the payment in wood and wheat. Credit was essential in the obtaining of imported goods from Montreal. The merchant would promise payment when he was reimbursed by his customers to whom he had also extended credit. If crops failed, if any dishonesty had taken place, or if the merchant had overstocked, he would not be reimbursed as expected, and would not be able to pay his suppliers. In the early stages of the developing economy, there was no fine or imprisonment for nonpayment of debt, and no interest was charged. The result could only be bankruptcy.

On the other hand, there were great opportunities for success. The merchant could quickly become a very influential and powerful member of the community should he exercise the options open to him. Since his was the only outlet for local and imported necessities, he could often set prices, and did. Since he knew everyone, he was often a middleman in business transactions, not likely to forget to reap his reward. With intelligence and luck on his side, he could not only expand his own successful business but also set up new businesses.

And as for activity: storekeepers have always had to lift, carry, sweep, dust, polish, arrange, count, and of course stand for long hours at a stretch. There were disadvantages for sure, but there was always the compensation of being at the centre of consumer activity, and of possibly being an independent, prosperous, and powerful man in the local world of village and town.
(*From* Illustrated Historical Atlas of Haldimand and Norfolk Counties, *1877-78.*) (*Opposite*)

BARTON BECKER.

Mr. Becker was born in the State of New York in the year 1800, and is therefore in his 77th year. He removed thence to the Township of Townsend in 1826, and entered the employ of the late Job Loder, Esq., with whom he remained three years. At the expiration of that time he removed to Rockford, in the same township, where he engaged in the lumber business quite extensively until 1837, when he returned to Waterford and was appointed Bailiff and High Constable, which position he held for five years.

About 1842 he opened a general store in Waterford, which he carried on successfully for twenty-seven years, and finding the premises he had occupied too small for his growing business, he built the large brick store which still stands at the foot of the main street near the bridge.

Being somewhat advanced in years, and having a competence, Mr. Becker then retired from business, and was succeeded by his son Leamon Becker, Esq., who has since carried on the business with ability and success.

Mr. Becker was married in 1828 to Miss Harriet Sovereign, and has had five children, three of whom are alive, one son and two daughters. Although Mr. Becker is now nearly 77 years old, he is still hale and hearty, and is one of the most respected citizens of the thriving village of Waterford.

LEAMON BECKER

Is the only son of Barton Becker, Esq. He was born in 1836 in Waterford, where he has since resided. Mr. Becker received a good education and entered his father's store as a clerk, where he acquired those business habits which have contributed to his subsequent success. In 1869 he entered into partnership with his brother-in-law, Mr. Foster, and began business as a general merchant in the store he now occupies; after two years Mr. Foster retired from the firm, and the business has since been carried on with unvaried success by Mr. Becker alone. He has added a tailoring department, and his stock of general goods is the largest and most varied kept by any merchant in the county, except perhaps one or two in Simcoe. Mr. Becker is shrewd and pushing, and has risen to be to-day one of the most enterprising, popular, and successful merchants in " Glorious old Norfolk."

Although the demands of his business make it impossible for Mr. Becker to hold any municipal or other public office, his means and influence are always freely employed in aid of any undertaking having for its object the social, religious, or material prosperity of the neighborhood in which he resides.

In 1864 Mr. Becker married Miss Mary F. Sovereign, a daughter of Leonard Sovereign, Esq.

Yours Truly
Barton Becker

RESIDENCE AND STORE OF **L. BECKER**, WATERFORD, CO. OF NORFOLK, ONT.

The General Store Today

In Southern Ontario a great number and variety of general stores have survived, many of which are being run as general stores, while others have been converted to other uses, such as homes, antique shops, craft shops, and small trade stores. They remain alive and thriving most often in small communities remote from urban centres, where local people are dependent on them, or on secondary highways where travellers stop for necessities. They are specifically located at the main crossroads of a village or on the main street of a once-burgeoning town. Though the general store is often discovered nearly unchanged, its surroundings have usually been altered over the years, as shops, houses, and taverns have been eliminated or transformed to suit modern needs.

In many cases, the general store is now solitary. For this reason it is difficult to imagine the general store in its appropriate setting and relationship to the nineteenth-century townscape. Some idea of the general store's place in the nineteenth-century town can be seen when visiting such towns as Bayfield, Cookstown, Niagara-on-the-Lake, Eden Mills, and Unionville. In order to enable people to see a general store as it appeared in the 1800s, several old stores have been moved to pioneer villages in the province, restored and stocked with items that were available and sold to settlers prior to 1900.

Most of the existing general stores documented in this book date from the last half of the nineteenth century.

Some stores have been changed only by time, some have been kept up or restored by successive owners, and others have been modernized to follow changing trends.

Rusty old signs, peeling paint, sagging wooden porches, rickety verandahs, and abandoned gas pumps are indicative of stores which have aged naturally. Though they may appear neglected, few are empty, and most are able to sustain a degree of trade.

Changes such as improved exterior wall covering, new paint, replacement of wooden porches with concrete, reinforcement of awning posts, removal of the upper balcony or lower verandah, and new signs are characteristic of stores which have been repaired and maintained over the years without altering the original character of the store building.

Relatively few stores which at one time had become dilapidated or had been converted to other uses, have been purchased in recent years by people with a personal interest in the old-time general store. These restorations often have duplicated the original appearance to such an extent that they resemble the restorations seen in pioneer villages. Two fine examples are to be found at King City and at Cookstown. Not all nineteenth-century general stores have been restored or remain original—there are many whose external appearance has been entirely altered by such additions as plate-glass windows, aluminum entrance doors, contemporary siding, and false-stone fronts. Verandahs, porches, awnings and other details have been removed. All of these changes have had the effect of diminishing the charm and quaint flavour, though these buildings still function as general stores.

The interiors of present general stores vary— quaint old interiors can be discovered, but many have been partially or completely modernized with dropped ceiling, flourescent lighting and standard metal shelving. Those that have remained unchanged inside display well worn wooden flooring, wooden wall shelving, a long, massive counter, glass and wooden display cases and other old store paraphernalia such as old cash registers, weigh scales, and cast iron rolled paper holders.

Best examples of interiors are in King City, Bethany, Cookstown, Denfield, Rosseau, Brookville, Rednersville, Damascus, and pioneer village stores. Some are lit by old hanging lamps giving the interior a very dim but extremely warm feeling. But all general stores whether modernized or virtually unchanged, have one thing in common: they are jammed with every imaginable article from hair curlers to chicken fencing and their interiors, although well organized, appear cluttered. Rummaging through any section of the store is always an interesting if not a learning experience.

Of the stores which are still operating as a general store, all sell groceries, but differ from the city corner stores in that their seasonal produce comes directly from the local farmers. Today, cheese, hardware and household items are sold in limited variety; brooms, rakes, oven mitts, dishes, farm equipment, utensils, limited

clothing and footwear, jackets, rubber boots, tee-shirts and underwear are included in the mélange. The modern equivalent of the general store with regard to the variety of items is Woolworth's, or Zellers, or Eaton's or an entire shopping mall. The types of goods are individually tailored to rural community needs. The one luxury not provided at the general store is choice. But it's more fun. Many shop owners do not clear out their stock. Consequently any article not in great demand, or overstocked, could sit on a shelf for many years, or be stored and put out at a later date. Some stores in the more remote areas sell unusual and interesting trinkets and clothing from the 1950s and one store near Kincardine had on its shelves in 1975 beautiful new satin bathingsuits from the 1940s in their original packaging.

The shopkeepers or owners of present day general stores are friendly and hospitable and enjoy their store and its customers. Most owners know all of their regular customers mainly because they have the time. It is not unusual to find two or three locals sitting around, drinking coffee, and talking to the storekeeper for hours while he continues to keep business running smoothly and tending to other customers. Getting together just to talk and enjoy company is a regular activity at some stores. A usual feature of country stores is a bench or a group of chairs where customers and friends can sit and chat while enjoying a pipe in pleasant weather. Such is the relaxed atmosphere of the general store in the more rural parts of this province. Compared with usual service at the city counterpart, one could easily see why people are drawn to the general store.

The shopkeeper's store is a popular centre of advertising. Often one finds announcements of the fall fair, lists of livestock for breeding, offerings of services, skates for sale, and notices of the community hall annual dance. Here much can also be learned of past history from the shopkeeper. He does not differ greatly from his nineteenth-century counterpart. In many cases he is the postmaster; he still offers home delivery and additional services related to community needs. His store remains a gathering place for customers to relax and exchange stories. The present-day general storekeeper never has to eavesdrop. He is in many cases everybody's friend.

(Preceding Page)
Mr. Turner serves a customer in his abundantly-stocked general store in Eden Mills.

A familiar fixture in the general store was the old stove. This cast-iron model is in the restored interior of the Doon Pioneer Village store. (Above)

(Right) With the introduction of the automobile, the general store offered yet another service—dispensing gasoline. This old gas pump is located in front of the general store at Argyle.

(Opposite) Damascus General Store.
With the increasing use of brand names, the exterior of the general store became a form of billboard advertising various products carried by the store.

What is to become of these charming stores which have survived to the present day in spite of changing times, in spite of urbanization of the countryside, in spite of progress?

Of those which still operate as old-fashioned rural general stores, many have been losing business over the past few years, while others are thriving. One owner, Mr. DesRoches of the Brookville General Store, says that the small general store has a future if it has the right location and satisfied customers. He feels that stock suited to the individual and particular needs of the local people and the provision of additional services such as home delivery and gasoline selling are essential to maintaining a regular clientele.

Large general stores such as Crawford Wells at King City and the store at Cookstown which carry a variety of goods and gift items and Canadiana-oriented stock enjoy a remarkable tourist trade mainly because of their proximity to Toronto. The store at Guelph is characteristic of a type of business which is actually on the increase. While it does not attempt complete authenticity in goods and services, it does provide some of the better elements of old-fashioned shopping such as unpackaged goods, a concept which is of growing appeal to today's customers.

But after witnessing the number of vacant stores, and stores for sale, and those general stores whose business is rapidly dying, the conclusion must be that many general stores in rural Ontario cannot compete with the growth of urban centres nearby, nor will they survive in their original capacity. Many general store buildings have been converted to other uses—the building still stands but its life as a general store, and the role it served in the surrounding community, have passed into history. One store owner, who now uses her infrequently-visited general store as a studio, sums up the predicament: "We just can't compete anymore."

Store at Baden.

The architecture is characterized by a fine sense of proportion and simplicity of design. Its wooden porch and stairs, its awning, and its simple carved supporting posts remain intact. It was last used as a tinware store, but was vacant when this photograph was taken in 1977. Dating from the mid-nineteenth century, this frame store is one of the oldest buildings in Baden. It is constructed of boards and battens. The lower windows were probably composed of many small panes like the upper windows but were replaced later by larger ones when they became available.

Present-day storeowner Gino de Luca relaxes in front of his general store in Aberfoyle. On an average Sunday in the summer months, he greets over two thousand customers, many of whom come to the village for the flea market.

(Lower) Some portion of the general store has always been used as a form of bulletin board relaying notices of local interest. Grahame's General Store in Bayfield still follows this practice.

The Stores

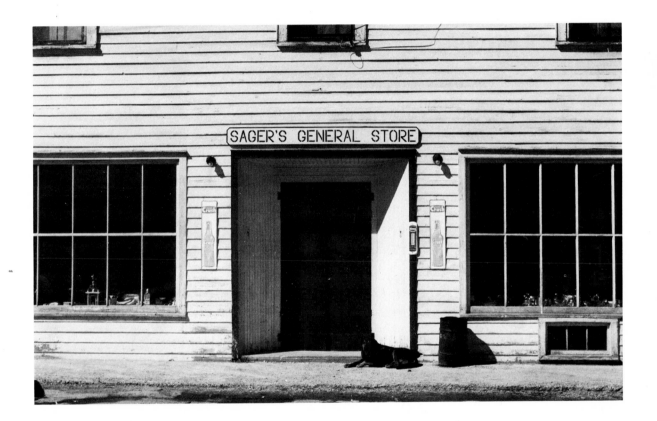

Stores That Have Endured

A local resident on the porch of the Country Store, Rednersville, oldest surviving general store in continuous use and on its original site in this province.

Kettleby General Store.

This store has been a village general store since it was first built in the 1850s and has changed hands many times in its 120 years. Its interior and exterior have been slightly altered, but it still maintains its role as Kettleby's only general store. It stocks mainly groceries now and functions as a convenience shopping place, though it is still the area post office. It is one of the few remaining stores to have preserved memorabilia of its early days: old account books, photographs and other interesting items such as an early twentieth-century scale which is still used to weigh produce.

Aberfoyle General Store.

In the past year the new owners of this store had the interior rebuilt by a local carpenter who modelled all of the shelves, counters, and storage bins on old designs. With its old weigh scales, its huge 1873 coffee grinder, and the smell of homemade pies and brewing coffee, this store has much of the charm of a nineteenth-century general store. It carries mainly food items and some crafts. Located on the main highway near the grounds of the flea market, it is an extremely busy place every Sunday in the summer. The building is reputed to be 147 years old. (Opposite)

Storekeepers

(Right) Susan Taylor, one of the storekeepers of the General Store in Cookstown.
(Lower) Bob Mitchell, former storekeeper at the Country Store, Rednersville.
(Opposite)
(Upper) Mrs. Robinson (right) and friends, Damascus General Store.
(Lower Right) The General Store, Doon Pioneer Village.
(Lower Left) Wilf McCluskey, Sheffield Country Store.

41

General Store, Bethany.

This tiny white frame store has remained virtually unchanged over the past fifty years. Behind the modest exterior lies a spacious and quaint store well-stocked with a variety of goods ranging from groceries to rubber boots. Situated on Highway 7 near Peterborough, it derives much of its business from travelling motorists. (Opposite)

The Corner Store, Claremont.

This general store is one of the most impressive buildings in the town. It is a monumental structure compared with most general stores and is constructed of orange brick with yellow brick used for emphasis of structural details. The front gable rises above the actual roofline and takes the form of a simple pediment, giving the building added height and prominence. The store's interior has been changed considerably—the shop occupies only half of the first floor. It now serves as a corner store stocking mainly groceries.

Rosseau General Store.

This store was built about 1870 and has been restored by its present owners, Mr. and Mrs. Tassie. It is an exceptionally large store with the rear addition and includes a butcher shop. The family's living quarters are in the house adjacent to the right side of the store. The customers are largely tourists and local folk.

(Opposite) A wide variety of goods can be found in this general store. Items are displayed on shelves, in old cases, on counters, and hanging from hooks and ropes. As well as carrying groceries and hardware, unusual items such as handmade mittens crafted by local people can be purchased here. Every bit of space is utilized to full advantage.

(Left) Mr. Tassie, country merchant.

The Country Store, Rednersville.

Established in 1803 by William and James Redner, the first Loyalist settlers in this area, this store has been in continuous operation for 175 years and is the oldest general store in Ontario. Constructed entirely of limestone, the upper portion of the front was replaced with red brick in the 1860s after lightning struck during an Orange Lodge meeting in the upper room, killing a man and his son. Today the store is still the focal point of the small village, functioning as a grocery store and gift and craft shop. (Opposite)

The Village Store, Halloway.

This beautiful brick and stone store was built in 1855 on what used to be the main thoroughfare between Belleville and Madoc. That same year a grist mill was erected across the street and operated in conjunction with the store. The store had been a familiar gathering place for mill customers and later a stopping place when the railway station was built. Often the attic of a store served as a makeshift inn for weary travellers. Later, Sunday school classes were held here.

Today it is called "The Village Store" and is owned by Mr. and Mrs. Haggerty. It is now bypassed by Highway 62; across the road, the old mill lies in ruin and the railway station has disappeared. The store carries some groceries and other staples, but on its shelves are the remnants of earlier days: stocking garters for men, bull and hog rings, horseshoe nails (five pounds for 49 cents), hat pins, and the old key to the front door; and outside is a rare find—double glass gas pumps from the nineteen-twenties.

McLelland's West End Store, Niagara-on-the-Lake.

Established in 1855 as a general store, it sold some exotic items such as Musk Oil, as well as groceries. Today the store's exterior remains original but has been covered with white paint. McLelland's is now widely known for its variety of quality cheeses, some aged to perfection. The smell of teas and other delicacies, the sloping wooden floors and low ceiling space with its beautiful hanging lamps, and the personal friendly service seem from another era.

(Opposite) The General Store, Cookstown.

The General Store, Cookstown.

This elegant store now owned by the Elchyshyns, has retained the name of a former proprietor, Will Silk. It carries a wide range of gift items and a limited assortment of candies, teas, spices, and cheeses. On weekends, throngs of enthusiastic shoppers crowd the aisles of this establishment. With its upper verandahed balcony, delicately carved wooden trim and imposing size, this store is one of the finest surviving examples of a mid-nineteenth-century general store in Ontario. Seen today, it has changed little since this photograph was taken at the turn of the century. (Lower)

(Opposite) The soft pastels of the interior decoration contrasting with the bright colours of the merchandise enhance the appeal of this store.

Crawford Wells General Store, King City.

Possibly one of the finest old stores in Ontario is this beautiful establishment. Built in 1863 (in what was once called Springhill) by Benjamin Lloyd, it changed hands several times, and in 1900 was purchased by James Archibald McDonald. The business was carried on by his brother John until 1914 when it was taken over by his son Wells, and a nephew, Crawford Wells. It remained in the Wells family until 1975 when it was sold. Its present owners have retained the name of Crawford Wells and have exercised great sensibility in restoring the building to its original appearance. It is now operated as a gift shop selling Canadiana and crafts and serving afternoon tea.

Although money was scarce in the early years of the nineteenth century, when it was in use no store was complete without its cash register and iron safe. This ornate register in Crawford Wells general store is similar to many found in old stores. The massive handpainted safe was usually found in the merchant's office. This fine example is found at the rear of this store.

An old bell at the front door of the store still alerts the shopkeeper when customers enter.

The interior of Crawford Wells is remarkably close in appearance to the interiors seen in turn-of-the-century photographs of stores of comparable capacity. Besides retaining its original wooden flooring and ceiling, this store is equipped with long stretches of wooden shelves, glass display cases, counters and cabinets. The profusion of appropriate and interesting paraphernalia from its past and present adds to the flavour of shopping in an old-fashioned general store of the past.

The polished stairway in Crawford Wells general store, King City, is unusually ornate and is a rare find.

Verandah at Crawford Wells. (Opposite)

Brookville General Store.

Situated on the Guelph Town line, near Eden Mills, is this 127-year-old general store. In its earliest days, it was a well-known stopping point on the footpath between nearby settlements and Hamilton where farmers travelled to have their grain ground. A tavern and stable was originally next to the store. Because of the village's notorious early history, Brookville and Haltonville, a few miles to the south, were referred to as Sodom and Gomorrah.

The building has always functioned as a general store, but three years ago, Mr. DesRoches purchased the store and has taken great care to restore it to its authentic old-time role. It is an old-fashioned general store in the true sense of the word. The stock is mainly determined by the customs of the local people. It carries a variety of goods: foodstuffs, including delicacies and homemade candies from nineteenth-century recipes such as horehound and butterpuffs supplied in old refillable jars by a local candymaker; hardware (nails, spikes, fencing equipment); drygoods, including overalls; snuff for a few special customers; new and used books.

Mr. DesRoches provides additional services: pumping gas, home delivery, and hauling. He believes that this attention to the specific preferences and needs of his customers is the essence of a successful general store.

There is a small degree of barter in items; local people bring in produce, such as chickens, and trade for other goods. And it still retains its function as the community advertising centre. This store is still an important social gathering place. Some of the long-time residents congregate at the store just to talk over old times. They also come to buy any piece of merchandise which they have become accustomed to and are certain they will find here.

The store's interior, although not completely authentic, has had its integrity preserved. It contains simple wooden supporting columns, the original flooring, and a long wooden counter.

The owner intends to continue his work enhancing the authenticity of his store.

Whitney's General Store, Morton.

This red brick store was established in 1850 by a Mr. Morton (the town was named after this prominent citizen). It has always served as a general store and is now owned and operated by Fred Whitney who has taken great care to preserve the authenticity of the interior.

Damascus General Store.

Very little remains of the village of Damascus except this little general store which derives business solely from local people. It is now situated in rural isolation. (Lower)

General Store, Arnstein.

Now a variety store, this establishment was built as a general store in 1901 by Julius de Bernardo, an influential citizen at the time. Julius and his daughter are seen in the store in this 1909 photograph, the property of the present owner, Ron Alder. Mr. Alder and his wife (opposite) have owned the store for the past 23 years. Its interior has been little changed in the past 75 years and retains most of its former charm, although time has greatly altered the exterior.

General Store, Duntroon.

This beautiful red brick store was built in 1873 and remained in the same family for 97 years. Seven years ago, Mr. and Mrs. Ford took over the business and discovered all of the original account books from the past century as well as unusual items which could be considered museum pieces. These articles, such as high-button ladies' boots and men's straw hats are now displayed on the original wooden shelves. The store also includes an old telephone dating from the early twentieth century which is not used but is still operable.

Although the Fords stock a limited selection of groceries, the store is used primarily as a workshop where Mrs. Ford teaches and makes lovely white clay ceramic pieces. The store, however, still functions as the local post office. In the past few years, the merchant trade has dwindled, and this store is one of many examples which have been pushed out by urban shopping centres.

General Store, Zephyr, a tiny store of austere beauty.

64

Country Store, Sheffield.

This business is still going strong according to Mr. McCluskey, the proprietor of this hundred-year-old stone country store. He says that on a "good" day he greets over two hundred people who pass through the front doors. The interior, though altered over the years, has one of the original pine counters and several glass and wooden display cases. Mr. McCluskey sells mainly groceries and household staples.

General Store Sprucedale.

After a fire destroyed the original store in 1939, this building was erected. Although its appearance is not as quaint as some old stores, it has a charming and spacious well-stocked interior and traditional friendly service. It is also a meeting place for local groups.

(Overleaf)
A patient horse awaits his master who regularly stops for supplies at Currah's general store in Gorrie.

Brubacher's Store, Elmira.

The original counters and shelving are still in use at this general store. The complete interior of this nineteenth-century store was removed from the original building on a main street of the town and relocated in Brox's Old Town Village, a new shopping complex with an old-time theme. The front door and shop windows from the old building were restored and incorporated into the design of the entrance.

Turner's General Store, Eden Mills.

This imposing limestone general store of 1871 dominates the main streetscape of the village of Eden Mills. It is a beautiful, austere building of unusual height and shape. It remains today little changed in appearance and in its role. Mr. Turner, its owner for 10 years, describes his stock in this way, "You name it, we have it." The interior, largely original, is packed with items of every description. It also carries an excellent supply of hardware materials, glass and fencing goods. The store includes a book exchange, a butcher shop with an elm block over seventy years old, the post office, and a collection of early Canadian artifacts collected by the owner and displayed in the windows and above the shelves. It is therefore a kind of museum. At one time the store was also a livery stable, and hay was stored on the upper floor and conveyed to ground level through a chute. This chute can still be seen at the rear of the store. (Opposite)

The Stone Store, Guelph (formerly the General Store).

A trip to the Stone Store in Guelph is, in many respects, like buying in a general store of the past century. It is unique because of the manner in which the goods are put out, selected, and carried away by the customer. Items such as twelve varieties of flour, beans, greens, nuts, dried fruits, dogfood, cereals, teas, and coffees are stocked in bins and barrels with scoops provided for the customers to measure out only the amount needed. Patrons bring their own jars and bags as the goods are not prepackaged. Shoppers are able to grind their own peanut butter from fresh peanuts which they scoop from a large basket. All purchases are weighed and priced at the 100-year-old counter. The store owners cater to the personal tastes of their customers and carry such unusual items as tofu and German health sandals. This Scottish-style limestone store was built in 1872 and has been a general store ever since.

A customer at the Stone Store in Guelph examines the goods.

(Lower)
Deep wooden bins holding cereals and other dry foods at this store.

Stores That Are Vacant

Not even a hint of its former bustle remains at the Country Store, Woodville, vacant and for sale in 1977.

The number of vacant and for-sale general stores in the province of Ontario indicates quite clearly the effect of urbanization of the countryside. The future of these stores is uncertain, although many have been rejuvenated and serve as specialty shops or general stores.

(Left) General Store, for sale, Rothsay.

(Lower) Interior of the Goodwood general store during a short period when it was unoccupied.

(Opposite) Vacant general store, Northport.

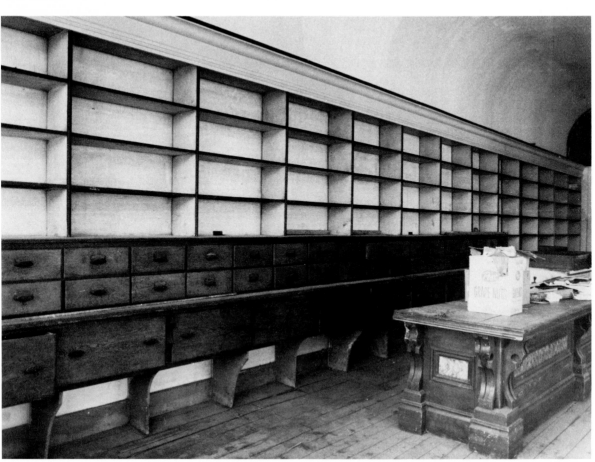

Shop windows, store at Goodwood. (Opposite)

General Store, Commanda.

Built in 1885, this store (overleaf) was originally on the old main street of the village but was moved in 1933 to its present site on the main road out of Trout Creek. It was owned and operated by Mr. George Hanselman until November 1977 when it was sold. The future of this remarkable store remained uncertain at that time. The profusion of decorative woodwork on the front facade makes this store especially noteworthy. It is one of the very few remaining examples having its upper and lower verandahs unchanged and untouched over the years. (Lower)

Rosser Store, Denfield.

West of London, in the tiny community of Denfield, is one of the most picturesque general stores in Ontario. Built in 1877, it was the village's first general store and shared its popularity with a hotel across the street and the railway station. It became the area post office in 1880.

The Rosser family took over the business in 1906. Mrs. Stewart Rosser recalls that in those days bread was four cents a loaf. The store also had a coal yard, and a telephone central (switchboard) located there was the first in the area. In the 1950s business declined, and the building became a storage shed until a related Rosser family purchased it for an appliance shop.

Today it is still owned by Frank Rosser. Although the store has not seen a customer in many years, it remains untouched and preserved. The interior contains many reminders of its past life—old newspapers dating back decades, high-button shoes, tins, and old signs. The weathered exterior, upper balcony, and shop windows and doors are all original. The spindly iron poles supporting the upper verandah have replaced the wooden posts which deteriorated many years ago.

(Lower) Rosser General Store as it appeared around 1900.

George Freeborn, son of A.F. Freeborn who owned the store in the 1940s recalls: "Believe me, that store had everything from pins to pianos and thread to threshing machines. . . . All the candies, cookies and crackers were delivered every ten days by a very nice man whom all the kids knew as "the Candy Man." . . . The hardware department had everything from carpet tacks to harness and hayfork rope—including cow chains . . . but the store also had a dry goods department. So if you'll step this way you will see that a man could be completely outfitted in work clothes from things in stock for about $12.

"Besides being a store it was also the focal point, recreation centre, and heart of the immediate community. People met to organize picnics, baseball teams and political campaigns. The Liberals would have it one night and the Conservatives for the next two.

"Somehow the people forgot to have a centennial for the town on its birthday so they used the birthday of the store as an excuse for a 'bash' last July (1977). . . . Unfortunately the old store was too old and too feeble to play an active part, but people did look at it and recaptured a lot of memories of the past. Some of them —memories and people—certainly captured me. I am and will remain their prisoner."

Former store building, Vivian is a fine example of general store architecture from the mid-nineteenth century. Its simple Victorian design is enhanced by charming decorative features such as polychromatic brickwork, ornate bargeboards (one missing) and the rounded arch motif of windows and the entrance door. This building was for sale when it was photographed in 1978.

(Opposite)

(Lower Left) The offer of a friendly cup of coffee conveys an ironic sadness. The once-thriving general store at Woodville was vacant and for sale in 1977.

(Lower Right) Years of exposure to the elements have defaced this old painted tin sign nailed to the side wall of the vacant general store building at Clavering. (Upper)

83

Nineteenth-century ornate cash register and old-fashioned coffee grinder in the general store at Doon Pioneer Village.

Laskay Emporium, Black Creek Pioneer Village, Toronto.

This store was built in 1845 by Henry Baldwin in Laskay. The town was founded in 1832 by his father Joseph Baldwin who had named it after his home in Ireland and who had established a saw and woolen mill there. Relocated here in the pioneer village in 1960, the store is a simple board and batten structure with a false front. The section on the left of the building was added in 1862 and here Mrs. Baldwin and her sisters conducted a dressmaking and millinery business. The shop is quite small, occupying the front of the main building with the post office in the back. Replicas of the kinds of items available in the 1850s, as well as some original items, stock the massive wooden counters and shelves and give an indication of the appearance of an original interior. (Opposite)

The General Store at Doon Pioneer Village.

This, an authentic general store built in 1836, was moved to its present site from Delaware, Ontario in 1961. Great care has gone into the restoration of both exterior and interior, making this store one of the most striking and charming of the museum-stores. Its exterior is typical of the modest nineteenth-century rural establishment, a one and one-half-storey house-like structure with gabled facade, large lower display windows, central double door and wooden porch. The lower facade is especially beautiful with its simplified pilasters applied at regular intervals. The handpainted wooden sign in the upper facade adds to its authentic appearance.

Entering the store, one initially wonders how an adequate supply of merchandise could have been stocked in this tiny interior. But the original pine counters are long and deep, the shelves extend from wall to wall and floor to ceiling, and many types of tools and utensils hang from hooks on walls and ceiling. Many articles which date from the mid-nineteenth century and which a rural store of that period displayed are presented in a way which is in keeping with the original arrangement of goods. Among the usual items, such as hats, textiles, tools, candy, soap, teas; there are appropriate furnishings: an old cash register, coffee grinder, and the familiar old iron stove.

Hay's Store, Muskoka Pioneer Village, Huntsville.

The restoration of this diminutive general store has been authenticated by the Museums Branch of the Ministry of Culture and Recreation. It was originally located in Falkenburg and was built in 1878. Its interior has been stocked with merchandise from the late 1800s: spices, notions, butter molds, apple peelers, carpenter's tools, and shoes.

General Store, Century Village, Lang.

This museum store was built in 1858 by a Scotsman, James Mather, in the hamlet of Menie near Peterborough. It remains unchanged except for the ceiling which was raised when the living space above it was no longer needed.

(Lower) Johnson's General Store, Fanshawe Pioneer Village, London.

This reconstruction gives some idea of the placement of the general store in an early nineteenth-century streetscape. The store has since been expanded.

Marsh's General Store, Coldstream.

Built in 1848 as a store and moved in 1869 to its present site, this seemingly-deserted building has become a restoration project of the St. Clair Region Conservation Authority. It has a traditional facade with pitched roof and gable front but has the main door located on a corner. This is an occasional but rare feature on surviving country stores in Ontario.

Bond Head saddlery was once the general store.

Store at Goodwood. (Opposite)

This building was formerly the village general store. Red and yellow brickwork on the facade forms a decorative pattern which adds texture and interest to the plain and rather austere structure. The design is enhanced by the simple and elegant treatment of the shop windows and main entrance door. It has recently become a speciality shop.

(Right) The former general store in Stouffville now serves as a rent-all for small machinery.

(Lower) Antique shop, Heathecoate, had a long history as a general store.

(Opposite) This outstanding building on the main street of Sunderland, while no longer functioning as a general store, still serves in a commercial capacity as a hardware and appliance store.

Shop building South March, formerly a general store, is now an art gallery and gift shop.

The Weaver and the Carpenter, Nashville.

Many former country stores of this type have been converted to serve a more contemporary market, although often their new names are reminiscent of former times.

(Opposite)

(Upper Left) Peck's store at Varna, once the general store, now sells appliances. This simple brick building is embellished by the still-intact verandah with its fine decorative wooden detailing.

(Upper Right) Kleinburg General Store photographed in the 1940s. It now houses the village post office. (Lower)

Acknowledgements

I wish to thank the storekeepers whose stores are represented in this book. They provided me with valuable information and countless cups of coffee. I would like to mention a few who were especially helpful: Gino de Luca, Aberfoyle; Mr. & Mrs. Ron Alder of Arnstein; Mr. DesRoches of Brookville; Marj, Mike & Kathy Elchyshyn of Cookstown; Mrs. Gordon Robinson of Damascus; Mr. & Mrs. Frank Rosser, and Steve Rosser of Denfield; Mrs. Ford, Duntroon; Mr. John Turner, Eden Mills; Brenda Aherne & Candice Pergolas of Guelph; Bill & Allyson Haggerty of Halloway; Mr. Carlson, Heathecoate; Andy, Doug & Marg Brookes of Kettleby; Mrs. Gail Rowe, King City; Fred Whitney of Morton; Paul Boyd, Bob Mitchell, Lorna Eberhardt of Rednersville; Mr. & Mrs. B. Tassie, Rosseau; Wilf McCluskey, Sheffield; Shirley McManus of Sprucedale; Douglas Pattmore of Stouffville.

I am grateful to those individuals who offered photographs to be included where needed: Ron Alder, Bette Gibson, Dan Leeming, Frank Rosser. Also, photos and information provided by pioneer villages especially Century Village, Lang; Muskoka Pioneer Village; Fanshawe Pioneer Village; and Province of Ontario Archives are greatly appreciated.

Lastly I would like to thank the people in the pictures for being there.

Photos not identified elsewhere:

Opposite title page: Aberfoyle General Store.
p. 5   At the Damascus General Store.
p. 8   Doon Pioneer Village.
p. 35   Sager's General Store, Queensborough.
p. 102   Shop window at Turner's General Store, Eden Mills.

Store Locations

All of the following locations are in the province of Ontario.

Historical Photographs and Sources